A VIEW FROM THE SOURCE

JEREMY HOOKER

A VIEW FROM THE SOURCE
—selected poems—

CARCANET NEW PRESS / MANCHESTER

Acknowledgements

My special thanks are due to Alan Clodd of Enitharmon Press: for his permission to reprint poems from two books originally published by him, *Soliloquies of a Chalk Giant* and *Landscape of the Daylight Moon*, and for his great practical encouragement.

Preface

This is a selection from my four books of poems: *Soliloquies of a Chalk Giant* (Enitharmon Press, 1974), *Solent Shore* (Carcanet, 1978), *Landscape of the Daylight Moon* (Enitharmon, 1978) and *Englishman's Road* (Carcanet, 1980). I have arranged it according to the periods during which the poems were written, and the dates given after each section on the contents page refer to these, and are not dates of publication. This procedure follows logically from my reconstruction here of my first typescript collection. *Landscape of the Daylight Moon* and *Englishman's Road* contain poems written between 1967 and 1973, and indeed there is nothing later than 1973 in the former. These poems together formed a large part of what I think of as my first 'book', and *Dedications* is a selection from that ghostly entity. The three sections that follow each represent a particular collection. I have omitted four poems from *Soliloquies of a Chalk Giant*, and the text appearing here is all of it that I wish to keep. My reasons for thus republishing it, with its integral note, are its particular character as a sequence, and the fact that it has for some time been out of print. The third section, *Solent Shore*, comes from the book of that name, and the fourth, *Under Mymydd Bach*, is a selection from the central section of *Englishman's Road*.

First published in 1982 by
CARCANET NEW PRESS LIMITED
330 Corn Exchange Buildings
Manchester M4 3BG

British Library Cataloguing in Publication Data
  Hooker, Jeremy
    A view from the source.
    I. Title
    821'.914   PR6058.0/
    ISBN 0-85635-379-5

The publisher acknowledges the financial assistance of the
Arts Council of Great Britain

Printed in England by Short Run Press Ltd., Exeter

CONTENTS

SOLENT SHORE (1973-76)

UNDER MYNYDD BACH (1977-79)

DEDICATIONS

A NOTE ON A POEM BY THOMAS HARDY

Today as you walk out, soaped raw
And rasped by Sunday fetters at the throat,
Too shy to speak, ashamed, yet proud,
Inclined at once to strut and feel a fool,
You bawl a greeting at your weekday mate
Behind the plough, and lightly on your sleeve
She laughingly remarks the sluggish toil.
A muttered recognition—all you need:
The knifed clods glitter as they fall,
Your awkward limbs start free
And swing in rhythm as her body flows.
And now your lordly gestures own the land
As she, submissive on your arm, looks on
Abandoned as the clay to manly things,
Until the rising smoke from distant fires,
Like summer taking leave in wisps of blue,
Breathes hazy sadness like a spice
And you go whispering by.

You would not notice, then, an ageing man
Who glances as you pass, nor care, perhaps,
That he should bear away from meeting you
An image of young lovers walking by,
A ploughman and the peaceful smoke
As things whose story will survive
Your children's children's end.

But what became of you he could not tell,
Nor whether, being universal, yet unwed,
You had no sons to feed another war,
Nor lay with her but with a shell instead.

THOMAS HARDY BURNING LETTERS

Commonsense does it.
First, bed it down, then rake over
Dry grass, dry sticks: that's the knack—
You don't know there's a breeze
Till it snatches; not too tight, though,
Or the match won't take.
That's it.
              Now the paper blackens,
Wrinkles like dead leaves, stains red
As the flames worm through.
It catches. And the heart blooms. Blooms,
And fails into smoke. The ash settles,
And you die as it dies, consumed.
There's only a pale film left, more delicate than petals.

They're all at it, gumbooted, sentinel,
Forking on weeds, trash, contents of attics.
You can see smoke standing up all over Wessex.

              Here's a man
Has a face only the mirror knows,
Who's watched himself burn there
And outstared the horror.
His pitiless scorched lip twitches.
I wonder, is that for a word
The fire glowed through
Before the heart crumpled,
Or because he sees
Scholars, years after,
Scrabble for ash on their knees?

EASTER AT WHITE NOSE

i.m. Llewelyn Powys

Over downland, where the field
Of wheat in an arc
Drops into space,
We find the clean-cut lettered stone:
THE LIVING THE LIVING HE SHALL PRAISE THEE

The chalk is a globe bitten
Through its axis, the white line
Of retreating cliffs
Jagged with marks of teeth.
Far up in the salt wind,

Hearing the sea crumple
Mouthing its stones, I could lie
Here like ash if death only
Meant contemplation
Under the gently reddening

Sunlight and salt.
Old atheist, the new corn
Has forced a green way
Through flints to the edge
Of your stone. Like St Francis

You have stretched naked
On the naked ground, thankful
At Easter for the unholy
Resurrections, and sure
There was no other.

These flints teach the same
Dogma, and the brute wheat
Supports you with its fine green
Shoots; perhaps it is only
A wish almost as old to sense
That I speak to a mind
In the smooth domed hill.

NOBBUT DICK JEFFERIES

('See'd ye owt on the downs?'
'Nobbut Dick Jefferies moonin' about.')

No one but him
Mooning in a backwater
Of the nineteenth century

We've walked apart from the houses
And here, on the edge
Of a common under pines,
Light in every facet
Dances round his words

Such tenderness
Is unbearable:
The point of a grassblade
On the eyeball

Even from the flowerhead
Of a slender foxtail, a branch
Grows over the earth's side
And he has stopped where it bends
Trying the body's weight
Against the bough's strength

The knowledge
Will not disclose itself,
Nor the world make something
Of him, though the extremity
Starts from its roots.

AFTER PAUL NASH

1

With my own eyes:
A brilliant transfer
So far at the back of the head
Bone hardened round it,

Cross and swastika,
A stack of fallen devils
With astounded eyes.

Later, a dead sea,
The brain's root jarred
By metal waves.

2

Reversion of a distant field
On a chalky swell
To the primal amoeba.

With nests of skeletons
Under her skin, the nursing stone
Takes back the bomber
Of nineteen forty.

The sun communes with the sunflower,
The moon haunts the daylight
Like the artist's eye.

ELEGY FOR THE LABOURING POOR

1 The Picturesque

'There will soon be an end to the picturesque in the
Kingdom.' (John Constable, after the destruction, by fire,
of Purns Mill.)

i

The picturesque is always with us.
Paint stiffens but the river swims forward;
Clouds move on and a mill becomes ash,
But the human features stay variable
And the pliant earth defies stasis.
And it is there, in that movement,
As another sky forms and a new generation
Measures the wood or levels the corn,
That the imagination commits itself
To an act that is elegy and salutation:
For what is welcomed—this continuity,
Is also change displacing the self that welcomes.
The carpenter alone commands a permanent living,
Elm perpetual usage. Nothing lasts
But the mortal nature of all that's unique.

ii

Near Bishopstone the family tended sheep
And ploughed the flint. There I glimpsed
A tractor fuming chalkdust
And found the fields worked profitably
But empty, smooth and pallid.
I came to the village under the downs
Whose graveyard held few stones—
The rest had ended in town cemeteries
Or been put to sea. Not one
Pushed a pen or was pushed by one.

Why grub in the past
For that life whose work seems fickle as ash?
Not to savour lachrymae rerum, nor toll
The general dirge that the globe goes round,
As the elegist wags a grave skull
Sonorous as a belfry: plough fossil,
Fossil pylon . . .
But to resurrect from the used land
The life that gave life; to utter it
As it cannot be known in the canvas
Where river and cloud stand fast,
Or in chronicles of the cold law;
As it can only be guessed by the self
Acknowledging change; as it can never be known.

2 *Forefather*

He moves like timber on a swell,
In mud gaiters and clay-coloured cord,
Bent to it, sculpting a furrow.
Mould's his name: James Mould
With shoots in Hants and Wiltshire.
His blunt boot-prints, fugitive
As the cloud at his rear,
Are unseen by the camera that exhumes
Celtic patterns from suave downland.
But the tread's purposeful.

His prayer's a bold harvest;
That the seed will stand up golden,
As an army, as mansions in Portland oolite,
As three loaves weekly.
God's ear is readier than Parliament's
Since He'll ferret in barn, byre and hen house,
Tithe hungry.
                    So he trudges
Chained by daylight

To the round of a stiff field,
Deaf as yet to saucy agitation.
For living it is not, but a long starving.

3 *'Gold Fever', 1830*

After nightfall in harvest weather,
Over the lowland clay
Where the axe has opened hearts of oak,
A faint wind moves in the rigging of leaves.
On the quayside at Poole
Limestone waits shipment, and Portland
With its moon-grey scars butts into the sea.
Bored by the company of sheep
White horses gallop on the ridge of chalk,
But the Cerne giant, erect through an aeon,
Dreams of slackening into repose.
—Green man, fathering riches,
Delicate in the turn of a leafy wrist
Or puckish among moon-drunk sheaves,
Subject to none but the turning year,
Now fires in the labourer's veins,
Kindling the brand—and flexes strongly,
In the fist that will quench it,
Musket and shot and the outraged warrant
Of a mastering brain . . .

No man's lonelier than James Mould
As he wakes with stubble-scored legs
In a rat's refuge of wattle and daub.
At first the mist hangs clammy flags
But vanishes as the sun hardens
White-hot on flint, deadening the hedgerows.
Hunger isolates: however neighboured
In a common circumstance,
The body slogs alone, by rote,
And the jailed brain dulls

Fixed on the single motion—the arcing scythe
Deliberate as the sun at its habitual act.
Thus he swings through the day, a young man
Hard and spare as the grain
Now whispering in heaps,
Bent with his shoulder to the field,
Keeping it moving, glad of the work,
At a Klondyke near Bishopstone.

4 *Captain Swing Fires the Workhouse*

Rag bedding indelibly staled,
Lousy straw crusted with piss—
Tinder for the pyre.

Lit, the flames flick cleanly.
Like a candle in a turnip skull
The house makes a face in the dark.
The grass slithers with rats.
Then the windows stare out,
Splintering, and the fire explodes.
To a shepherd out on the downs
It's a cauldron fed by the oak,
As it ruins suddenly, lustily,
And the walls wither and the roof falls,
Pounding down timber and stone.
Like a yule log
It flickers on the watchful old.

Where's Swing?
The sergeant barks at his redcoats.
The magistrate chokes on latinate prose.

No one knows.
Not even a score of labourers
Cat-footing it through the underwood;

Among them, James Mould,
Daredevil as a boy again,
Pleased with himself and scared.

5 *The Voyage Out, 1831*

Bladder-wrack swaying in supple knots
Muddies the sunned quayside water.
Each for itself and each self
Viciously alike, the black-headed gulls
Snatch at refuse and their raw cries
Spread in circles, smacking the hulk,
Thinning out where the estuary opens
And the sea absorbs their voice.
But James Mould seeing the ocean
Sees only flint acres
Fought inch by inch, chalkdust rising,
And hears only his ghostly kin
Telling their names in the stunned brain.

When Portland pitches astern
And the last gull's torn shoreward,
Memory stays. The hulk bores on,
Shuddering, and the massive slabs break,
The clean fathomless wells slide open.
But the waves have faces
And the unbroken space narrows
To an inland patch of fields,
The chalk ridge, the sheep-walk scabious.

For this is purgation: to scour men
By divorcing them from all they know.
But the things they love go with them,
Untouchable, at times ferociously clear.
And what's left pleads after them,
And sours. Places are empty
That nothing but bitterness can fill.

The labourer voyages. The land uses
New methods, new men. But he takes with him
A life belonging to those acres
And leaves as a portion, the emptiness.
Under the downs, in countless sites
Gutted by the exile of their people,
Others will meet this isolation.
They will inherit the emptiness.

ALL RIGHT

I walk by the window.
My reflection wavers in the glass,
But within, in shadow,
Across the stillness of the room

Where you kneel with a book
By the fire, you look up and
I see your eyes at once brighten
At the centre of my gaze.

The half-light swirls
From your mouth's inaudible
Welcome. Between us I know now
That it is all right for ever.

BIRTHDAY

When I wake, you are standing
Beside me. In the icy Victorian vase
Decorated with glass-cut fern,
You bring catkins, silver-grey

Pussy willow, and snowdrops.
A fine yellow powders your hand.
It is late March, the cold earth
Is broken and out of darkness

You bear a gift. I marvel, love,
To have been born for this.

THERE

As sett to badger dark in the warm soil;
As moist places to the secret mole;
As essential darkness to earth itself:

Love, the night surrounds us.
We are the confluence of underground streams.
We grow together and in daylight
Flow out apart, now each in each, remade.

WASPS

Mad for nectar still,
Dying wasps crept everywhere.

They blundered against the windows
And spun on invisible pins,
Stunned by coldness we did not feel
Though the sun shone whiter
At a different angle.

I remember the beginning for its peace,
Blue autumn's blood-drowse cooling,
Agitated by the pitiful anger of wasps.

EARTH POEMS

1 Song of the Earth

Bring or do not bring your mind's distress.
The seas it foundered in
Are none of mine.

My words are flint, cold to your touch.
They tell I am
What you become.

No tree bore the branch
From which your sick thoughts spin.
There is no vertigo in falling leaves.

Along brain's empty dancing-floor
My small blades creep.
The grass's flood-tide bears you home.

2 At the Edge

You will haunt the edges
Becoming more shadowy the more
This world streams past.
Now there is nothing but grassblade
Running into grassblade,
Each a separate wave where the colours flux
Orange into brown. The field is going out
With the autumn tide,
And where you were there is now
Only a cry.

3 The Elements

Even a poor eye
Can see clear through the globe

To its Antipodes. All, all,
Like a frail door banging in the wind,
A leaky raft through which the sea springs,
Cannot keep out the other elements.
With faculties so weak
You can reach out to touch the other side of death.

LANDSCAPE OF THE DAYLIGHT MOON

I first saw it inland.
Suddenly, round white sides
Rose through the thin grass
And for an instant, in the heat,
It was dazzling; but afterwards
I thought mainly of darkness,
Imagining the relics of an original
Sea under the chalk, with fishes
Beneath the fields. Later,
Everywhere upon its surface
I saw the life of the dead;
Circle within circle of earthen
Shells, and in retraced curves
Like finger marks in pale sand,
The print of a primaeval lover.
Once, climbing a dusty track,
I found a sunshaped urchin,
With the sun's rays, white
With the dusts of the moon.
Fetish, flesh become stone,
I keep it near me. It is
A mouth on darkness, the one
Inexhaustible source of re-creation.

LANDSCAPE OF THE WINTER SUN

The sun, over the ridge,
Refines its stony bulk
To an airy whiteness.
Light glancing draws the eyes
Upwards, to the centre;
But a glimpse closes them.
When sight clears, there are
Fiery points in irregular patterns
Across the field; in intricate
Bare hedges blackthorn leaves
Edged with ice; distances
Where, in a few months,
None will exist. For a time
It is as if the sun looks
At a landscape it has
Simplified, until, standing
On a bank for the view,
I am surprised by a shadow's
Comical stick-like elongation
Spanning a small field.

TO A WELSH POET

1
Death
Stiffens
The green limb.

The power men make
Makes them powerless,
For a time:
A charred corpse

Burnt in the steelworks,
Is a furnace of anger,
Resistance, pain.

2

A small man, around
Him the granite walls
Of Dartmoor.
His jailors face away
Listening for gunfire
In a corner of Europe.
And he is sustained,
On this front,
By the secret passages
Of speech.

Not one man, but many,
Living and dead,
Stiffening
In corrupted ground.

3

He was on the far side
Of another language,
An old man I never spoke to,
In the next room.

Five years later,
Facing deep into England
I could ask him:

Teach me now
To speak to the living.

LANDSCAPE

1 Rock and Fern

Inches away a beck slices the hill.
Catching my breath, I rest under the last thorn.
After it there's nothing green,
Only smooth stones, russet scrub,
And among the whin, rough stones.
But here, on a rock blanched by it,
The sun prints the shadow of a fern,
Still as a fossil, pointed like an arrowhead:
The mottoed tablet to an aeon.
A breeze jigs the fern,
And between moments of perfect white
The rock flickers. Then the wind stops
And the fern stiffens, a shadow bedded in rock.
Feeling invisible, I climb on.

2 Rock and Water

The beck strikes down,
Jabbing wittily through narrows,
Stopping to consider a slow pool
And sliding out cleanly over domes of rock.
At a bend the air decays,
Rotting for yards beyond the carcass,
Bone needles stuck through a mess of wool.

Bleached pates of rock, shreds of foam
Dull beside quartz, the sunstone glittering.
At intervals, unscoured rock piles
Keep a quiet like sacked monasteries.
And everything's hot to touch.
My shadow moons in a pool
Or lies crooked and breaking in shallows;
Delicately, a trout flicks through its head.

3 At the Source

Sheep jump up around me,
Their long skulls chock with horror.
The hills have heard little but bleating
Since the glaciers went by.

But I forget the pipit
Startled by my drudging boots, wrenching the eye
Upwards, the gaze beaten back
But for an instant free of spaces
Where a separate music's made.
I forget many things, mainly things:
The multiple unreckoned differences.
In the heat my hands swell and flush
Tightening the ring on my finger.

At the source
The mean bitten grass becomes mush,
Reddish-brown, with islands of moss.
But I cannot call it the source.
The beck's been fed all the way
By others of equal size.
This one's no bigger than a puddle:
A small clear pool with a hint of iron.
I breathe over it, earthbound and aching.

The hills bleat.
The pipits address miles of air.

4 A View from the Source

The century drew out
Freighted with ore, jolting upline,
To stake with a bayonet acres of dead.

It had served; it could fail,
Poison the beck, and the beck

Empty its puffed white fish on the sea;
The place gutted, forgotten.

I can imagine the dark dispelled
By prosperous light; miners break earth;
All that's impossible
But ghosts in a place so dead.
A stone pitched in the shaft
Plummets from hearing with a metallic ring.

SLEEPING OUT ON PEN CAER

for Peter Clarke

We are not mystics
Though this was their country:
Crested headlands
Like stone dragons drinking,

Haunt of hermit and guillemot;
Swirl of white islands
Where the current bore them,
Crucifix for pilot, among the seals.

We could have had a warm bed,
But chose discomfort, cold,
Feeling the earth
With our bones, under
The immense pale drifts of the Milky Way.

We have our whisky and tobacco.
We belong as much to jets
That pass above, as to the stars.

Before light the gulls' cries
Wake an older earth; hoarse and shrill,
The salt cry of rocky islands.

The sun appears, a red ball
Over the volcanic crags
Of Garn Fawr.

Out at sea the esses of a breeze
Lie like the marks of a lash
Flicked on a smooth insensible hide.

TO THE UNKNOWN LABOURER

No monument
For time to smear;
No statue
That a man conceives
To trap himself in stone.

Only earth
Where a night's rain
Washed out his prints;
Chalk where his life
Was moulded;
Fields like hands after work,
Rough palms spread.

SOLILOQUIES OF A CHALK GIANT

I was with the first inhabitant
In these hills and I stayed here
After him, at the foot of his grave.

MATRIX

A memorial of its origins, chalk in barns and churches moulders in rain and damp; petrified creatures swim in its depths.

It is domestic, with the homeliness of an ancient hearth exposed to the weather, pale with the ash of countless primeval fires. Here the plough grates on an urnfield, the green plover stands with crest erect on a royal mound.

Chalk is the moon's stone; the skeleton is native to its soil. It looks anaemic, but has submerged the type-sites of successive cultures. Stone, bronze, iron: all are assimilated to its nature; and the hill-forts follow its curves.

These, surely, are the work of giants: temples re-dedicated to the sky god, spires fashioned for the lords of bowmen:

Spoils of the worn idol, squat Venus of the mines.

Druids leave their shops at the midsummer solstice; neo-phytes tread an antic measure to the antlered god. Men who trespass are soon absorbed, horns laid beside them in the ground. The burnt-out tank waits beside the barrow.

The god is a graffito carved on the belly of the chalk, his savage gesture subdued by the stuff of his creation. He is taken up like a gaunt white doll by the round hills, wrapped around by the long pale hair of the fields.

FOUND OBJECTS

1
A reindeer bone carved
in the reindeer's likeness.
Saddle-quern
Loom-weight
Spindle-whorl.
A chalk phallus.
A lump of chalk
with heavy curves bearing
the image of woman.

2
A necklace with blue beads
of Egyptian faience, black ones
of Kimmeridge shale.
Slingstone
Cannon ball
Cartridge.
A phallus carved on the church wall.
A statuette of the Virgin.

3
A coin worn headless,
with a disarticulate horse.
Cartwheel
Crank-shaft
Flash-bulb.
A bust of the death-god
cast in imperishable alloy.

FOSSIL URCHINS

A tribe found them, believing
They grew like dandelions
In the soil.
          An exquisite
From the Age of Fishes
Became the sun's icon,
                    crowned with rays,
And a ring of suns,
Sacred to the resurrection,
Was placed around the dead.

There is still
A touch of man.
They are composed
Of blood and fire,
Where the sun roots in the earth.
They are not clammy like potsherds,
But shapely, and warm to the hand.

FLINTS

They are ploughed out,
Or surface under surface

Washes away leaving the bleached
Floor of a sunken battleground.

Some are blue with the texture of resin,
The trap of a primeval shadow.

Others are green,
A relic of their origins.

The white one is
An eye closed on the fossil.

Worked in radial grooves
From the bulb of percussion

They shed brittle flakes.
The core with its brutal edge

Shaped the hand.

THE AGE OF MEMORY

It is over three hundred years since the churchwarden paid
a carpenter three and tenpence for converting the maypole
into a town ladder.

The puritan is a good toolmaker. He contracts his work-
force from the boozy remnant whooping in the ring.

Even a backwater is shaken by purposeful tremors,
when it empties. Afterwards, the place is greener. The
native god is exposed for the first time.

If the god is a spectacle, he is no longer blind. In the
scheme of things he becomes guardian of the dead. He is
invested with memory. The insignia of office is an invisible
globe.

THE INVISIBLE GLOBE

On bare hillsides, pale fields,
History was a story indeed,
Of labour and conflict
And prayer; now remote
Like a stranger's dream.

Labourer, monk,
Each singular one:

They have abandoned the place
To contemplation;
The cloisters have merged
In silence deeper than prayer.

But to the chalk there is
One human fact in the landscape
The landscape can share:
All the dead
Contract to a single bone.

Chalk, too, has its dream.
Of the bone
On a white ground
Of endless beginnings.

SOLILOQUIES

TOTEM

Where are the giant's people?
They have followed the mole
Under mounds. The Dance
Is a ring of stones.

Soon there will be nothing
But a breeze gathering dust
Over pale fields, a maze
Of ditches scored on the hill,

Unless a man stand naked
Of all but imagination.
Let him discover me.

I rise through him
Or lie here and wait,
Scratched in the chalk.

THE GIANT'S BOAST

I was before Christ, and I remember
The saurian head of my begetter.
I conceived these words at my creation,
When you traced your shadow on the stone.

I was before Moses, and his fury
Returned me to the elements,
From which I am remade.

I have walked with my ribcage naked,
When the strong man dug his grave.
I have contemplated the skeleton
Under the flesh of all things,
And I gave to the holy waters
A natural potency.

The smoke from a wicker basket
Was sweetest to my nose;
For I have levelled and engendered
Multitudes, and I do not answer
To a single name.

No man understood me
Who called me brutal, and no woman
Who called me kind.
Mothers and daughters worshipped me.
I worshipped with my body
The naked ground.

THE GIANT'S SHADOW

I am the giant who carries a giant
On his back.
This is my comrade.
Is he alive or dead?

I stoop and cry out,
Let go, let go.
When I look up
The shadow hangs over me
With crossed wings . . .
Impure fancies, how they breed
In the sludge
Of a standing mind!

Do you imagine the dead stop in their graves?
Stones of the abbey that vanished
Are mounted on my spine.
This is history,
When the mind is an open grave.

You are sunlight,
You are darkness,
Green god.
The rest is illusion.
Illusion with talons hooked through my bones.
It is an anchor
From the bottom of the sea,
It is fixed in the floor of the sea
Like an axe-head fast in a skull.
If I could move it, the world would shift.

How heavy the shadows are!
I wrestle with them all day long,
Fingers clutched round my cold stave.

EARTH-BORNE

Though they called my people
Dwellers by the water,
I am no sailor, least of all
A Celtic saint.

Far from the sea, too far,
I am nostalgic for their lives,
For the green sea of darkness
And beaked wave.

Where the wind and tide quarry,
And in an instant smash,
The green-veined slabs of stone,
They give the tiller to the tide,
As if provided for.

No sons of Aphrodite, shell-borne
Zealots gaunt as your stone cross,
The wandering limpet knows its home.
I am too much your opposite:
Earthbound, as if the earth
Were not a sea.
My fingers, bloodless, white,
Are knotted to a stick I cannot drop.

THE GIANT'S CLUB

It was here from the first,
An oak branch,
Shaped like a leaf,
Growing from my hand.

I am a man
Carved from an oak
Traced on a stone
Cut in the chalk.

Why do you lie to me,
Setting giant
Against giant,
One savage, with the club

Of annihilation,
Which the other evades?

It is I, whom you call
Priapus, who bear the club.

If it rots
It is not a limb
To amputate.
Without it, I fall.

Phallus and club are one ground.
Terror is their separation
In the mind; the other face
Of terror, your indulgent smile.

WHAT IS A GIANT MADE OF?

I have seen myself
Standing defiantly
Apart from the hill,
And I have seen,
Through earth's tissue
And a sky
Without foundation,
The daylight moon,
Brittle as a chalk fragment,
Reflecting my disdain.

What is a giant made of?

There is a clump
Of flowering blackthorn
Spattered with the dung
Of rooks: these, too,
Are the giant,
These white flecks.

There my eye sleeps
With its mirrors turned
To the wall of my skull,
And beneath me
I feel the grass rise
And fall, like the slow,
Deep breaths of a giantess.

A CHALK PEBBLE

This is perfect:
A chalk pebble,
Smooth and round,
Like an egg
With the foetus
Of a giant
Curled inside.

When I touch it,
My hand crumbles.
The hill is a fine cloud
Whitening the Cretaceous sea.

Starfish, urchin, spunge,
I have become many:
We do not trespass here,
Composed on the white floor.
We are not foreign to this ground.

Who is the saurian
Tyrannizing the shallows,
Smashing a trackway
Through the new green trees?
His familiar,
Disproportionate head
Is small and mean.

The giant turtle is in its element,
Housed on the summit
Of low white hills.
The dead spunge mingles
With alchemic water
For the slow formation
Of a perfect stone.

CHALK MOON

How it leeches the mind,
When a daylight moon rises
Like a piece of the hills.

There is no darkness here;
The living are so remote.
Even the club feels powdery,
Crushed in my hand.

The sea has withdrawn far out;
Streams cannot reach it.
They die of thirst
In a landscape picked to the bone.

When the wind blows
My breath tastes of dust.

ONE FLESH

I raise my arm
And the club's chalk stem
Branches from my hand.

I kick out my legs
And the phallus extends
Like a belemnite.

I force a passage
In the shape of my body
From the chalk,

And emerge offensively,
Brandishing weapons,
About to shake off the dust.

THOSE WHO HAVE NOTHING

They still seek me,
Those who have nothing.
Others consume their plenty
And look away.

They watch as the night grows colder.
They breathe on the clenched hill.

I take from them
A little warmth
And carry under my ribs
The impression of bodies
Formed in the dew.

THE PROTECTOR

I was made naked
To protect men
From evil spirits.

I was given a club
To protect them
From the tangible.

When the ghouls whicker
Around my nakedness,

Exchanging sex and club,
I become their reflection
And they rot.

DAWN

There is a moment
No one sees,
When earth is formed
In the image of neither
Mist nor light.

Grey flowers grow
On the giantless hill,
Over the untouched graves.
Sleeper and sleepless lie
Without a name.

Colour breaks and this day
Is one of the millions,
Bloodred, gold, with a streak
Of unearthly green
Like the eye of a god.

Dawn is perfection
Of a kind. Now I wake
To the unfinished act
And the dead lie complete
For ever, under their names.

THE MOTHERS

I know this land: it was made
In the image of the Mothers.
Even now it makes me sick,
Living on a roller that never breaks.

It is white under the plough, and so smooth
The eye cannot stand.
It is always winter here
And the moon looks down, pleased.

I was made to stand against this,
A rude bulwark the grass ignores.
Every man is a defiant boy
Defiling the tits of a giantess.
He is drowned many times over
In his own seed.

Man's image of a man:
Stone Age and omnipotent,
Subduing with two weapons:
After brutality, tenderness . . .

Even the chalk is female.
It has not stopped laughing
For two thousand years.

DEVIL

Who was the goat upon hindlegs
Who tickled with a whiskery thigh
The hairless monk?

When the young friar drowsed
I drew with his goosequill in the margin
Pictures of beasts and birds.

He saw a devil to castrate,
Initialed in God's name between my legs,
Jehovah Destroyed This.

Though weather rubbed it out,
This was God's patent for the age.

I am the pupil of the eye,
Diminished by a cool, bored look.

MOTHER AND CHILD

One in the earth
Crouches, a skeleton
With a skeleton
In her arms.

The other
On the tower
Chills me with her purity,
Draws me to her warmth.

I listen to the silence,
Leaning down
From the crumbling arms
Of the hill.

ABORIGINE

Streams dig with their flints.
Chalk rises through stubble
Like a moon. From this page
I learnt my name.

Everything refers me back
In time. Chalk words. Flint words.
The chalk are porous, and crumble.
The flint are hard.

I am bound to the place
By its language.
I was taught to speak
In such metaphors.

When I am dead the language
Will shed me. Till then
It takes something of me
Wherever it goes.

THE GIANT'S FORM

What does the child scrawl
On the smooth flat top
Of a tomb?

Augustine's well,
With cold green lights,
May spring through flint.
Here, within
The burial ground,
He thrust his staff
Into the earth:
                    I see God!

Now let the saint
Give back his halo
To the sun, and to the earth,
Adopted sanctity;
For should the grass
Grow through my sides,
The playing fingers
Of a child
Would still depict,
With blind recall
On some flat stone,
The giant's form.

YELLOWING MOON

The rotted flints alone
Are motionless. They lie
In half-light, blue scars
Touching, under the barley.

Hardly a patch shows white.
Shadow softens the glare
Of tracks. These are nights
Of the yellowing moon.

Now fire-tints melt
Enclosures, run fields together
In one broad curve
Of ripening grain.

A pigeon flaps away;
Heat-haze resolves it
In a dozen yards
Into a burr of energy.

Nothing is self-contained.
There is no standing apart,
Of tree, or barn, or man.
I am possessed like a single stalk.

THE SIREN

Death, too, is a profession.
It has its orders and degrees.
The finality
Of an inscription
Exalts the hand.

Tympany of the Nordic storm-god,
Basso profundo, tumid with doom.

On a pipe made from swan's bone
The siren always plays
Her softer airs.

ELEGY FOR THE GIANTS

Scorn broke them; they softened,
Mouldering like touchwood.
An effigy found in an attic,
Lugged out to be burnt,
Was once the molten god.

Beggared Herakles became a clown
And as the clodpole with a stave,
Beelzebub, invited blows
And laughter. They bragged
And bluffed and roared,
Jaws gored with rouge,
Exalting some boy-hero
By their fall.
Like Ysbadaddan,
All were well shaved.

Others turned to stone.
They wear grey habits
With an austere dignity.
They are upright, with ascetic faces.
They have fallen and do not plead.

MOCKERY

Though delight fails me and the will dies,
I am the involuntary prodigal.
As always I sign myself
Your obedient servant
And because all things bear it
My name breeds contempt.

Here the migrant renews its cycle,
Here the young goat shivers
And foliage greens the naked horn,
Here the old track starts from the source,
From here it is never the same.
It is through me, always.

I laugh at conceptions of genius.
With mockery the fool announces his birth.

THE SPRING

Let there be peace between us,
Tortured god.
Like a lesser sun,
The light of your church
Once cast my shadow.
I sprouted horns
Like a Lord of Beasts.

I am no longer strong
In my strength;
And you, no longer strong
In your weakness,
Can you accept this water,
Once sacred to me,
That your blessing cursed?

STASIS

I strain to reach downwards
Out of the glare.
I am closed out.
Dust seals my mouth.

Nothing moves
But a glittering point
Scratching a chalk track
Across the sky.

Every surface reflects
My lifted arm.
If I could move
I would destroy them.

Failure does not teach me patience.
When I am exhausted,
There is a gust of darkness,
A smell of water on the air.

SOLSTICE

Is the poppy afraid
Of its redness?
I am not a dry leaf
That flares to nothing.

Roots drink at my side.
Chalk absorbs my warmth.
And still I am replete,
Blood-ripe.

The facets of every flint
Glow red. No surface
Remains unkindled
To reflect my stare.

All day sun passes
Through me.
I am burned on the hillside
With its brand.

PRAYER IN WINTER

Give me courage, hunter,
When energy has bled down
To the roots and the moon
Is a chalk pebble hurled
Into the sky, when rain
Turns dust to sludge
And the wind hacks my groin.

Give me the courage
Of your slow retreat
From the frozen springs, following
The signs of reindeer and bison.
When life retreats, let me
Follow the signs.

HEIL

Heil, they shout. *Heil.*

Wolves are my kinsmen.
Beneath each wolfskin,
A guttural peasant.

Heil, Heil.

They deafen the oracle
With their shouting.

Heil, Heil.

How shall I defeat the darkness
I am part of?
The hero gores himself
Wrestling the dragon.

THE GIANT'S NAME

In which district the god Helith was once worshipped.

Here, in darkness, come the humble members of Christ's body. *In quo pagim* the risen Christ gleams; but Helith smoulders, reddened by the peasant's breath.

Our high admiral Hercules.

This is the ship of England, carved from a single oak. Her master is navigant of the obscure passage, a hard-headed merchant with a fabulous map. He descends into the pit, and wrestles with the furnace. His labours are wrought in iron.

Helith; that is, holy stone—or a corrutpion of Helios, the sun? A sunstone, pediment in earth. The ground is dense with holy names: Elwood, Elston Hill, Elwell, Yelcombe *(y el cwm)*. Was there a standing stone on Elston Hill before Helith was fleshed out below the Trendle? *Where beth they, beforen us weren?* Make your enquiry of the dust.

I make no enquiry there. Give me a living name.

A WIND OFF THE SEA

It exhausts me at last,
This querulous petition
Of a chalk Hamlet
To the ground.

The sea-wind needs
No addition from complaints;
It has touched
Chert and flint,

Left the smooth boulder
Unmoved, but acquired
Something of the character
Of stone. I leave

My mouth as its portion.
Let it resolve my breath
Into a taste of salt,
A scent of thyme,

A touch of stone.
My image I leave
To whoever it reflects;
But my body is the sea's;

It is a piece broken
From the hill, a chalk
Stack, not formed,
But worn down by the tides.

A NOTE ON THE GIANT

To anyone familiar with the original, it will be apparent
that the figure of the chalk giant is based on the Giant of
Cerne Abbas.

   The Cerne Giant is an impressive figure, assertively phallic
and caught in an instant of dynamic movement, as if in the
act of tearing himself from the hill with club raised, and
frozen there for as long as he exists. The arrested energy is
all, the image of a giant about to leap, to beget and to de-
stroy, of a man who is not quite a man, who is perhaps less
and perhaps more, whose flesh is not quite flesh . . . The
statistics are not vital, but do have a bare suggestiveness.
About 25 tons of turf, soil and chalk were removed at his
creation; he is 180 feet tall (200 with the club, which is
120 feet long) and the phallus measures 30 feet.

Awareness of chalk and flint coincides with my earliest impressions, but I have known of the existence of the Cerne Giant for about ten years and once lived within his ambit. In this period I have often visited Cerne and have read all that I could find relating to its Giant. One of the most impressive facts to emerge from such a study is, in one sense, a negative one: very little is known, and nothing for certain, about the origins of the Giant. Here, all is speculation and there is little to choose, except in inherent probability, between the inspiration of the romantic who tells himself a story about how the Giant came to be on the hillside and the theories of the expert. Folklore has a David-and-Goliath tale in which a boy captures the Giant when he is sleeping off a glut of local sheep; it is an old tale, but new in relation to Helith.

One writer argued for a comparatively recent date, in the seventeenth century, when he believed the figure to have been cut by servants of the Royalist, Lord Denzil Holles. In my view this theory shows obdurate insensitivity to the Giant as the embodiment of a particular quality of imagination, implying a particular society, and lack of historical sense in ascribing a work of art to a period that could not possibly have produced it. The Giant's pronounced sexual characteristics, to say nothing of their relation to his ferocity, in a figure that emphasises, above all, the connection of procreative and destructive powers, are surely the attributes of a fertility god, not of a half-mocking, wish-fulfilling image of lechery in the mind of a follower of Charles II—or of his servants, even if they were men of the Maypole. Perhaps the seventeenth century rediscovered Helith after a period when his outline merged with the grass, after the dissolution of the abbey.

Another writer has argued for a date that would make the Giant roughly coeval with the beaked-horse of Uffington, in the Celtic Iron Age. Certainly the head of the Cerne Giant does bear a remarkable family likeness to a head of the Early Iron Age, c. 200 B.C., depicted on a tin-plated brass plaque from Tal-y-llyn in Merionethshire. In this head, in the Uffington Horse-goddess, and in the stylised horses which become increasingly disarticulate on Celtic coins, one can see, with no expertise at all, the lineaments of an ancient symbolism which is now, like Helith, open to a variety of interpretation.

A great deal of recent expert opinion affirms, but cannot confirm, the Giant's Romano-British origins, perhaps in the second century A.D., when the worship of Hercules was revived by the Emperor Commodus, who believed himself to be a reincarnation of the god. From a purely aesthetic point of view, it certainly does make sense to see in the Giant's appearance a confluence of Celtic and Roman influences. One writer in the nineteenth century called him 'Baal Durotrigensis' and the affirmation of a Celtic origin, as a totem of the Durotriges (dwellers by the water), or of an earlier people, is true to his appearance, which also suggests that a Roman thought went to his making. Whichever view one takes of his age, it seems probable that he was not the first giant on the site, even if, in an earlier incarnation, it was a standing stone.

Undoubtedly Cerne has been one of the holy places of Britain from very early times and the alleged mission of St. Augustine, who is said to have seen God there and thus named the place (*Cerno El!*), or the actual mission of some other Saint, had to contend with a primeval tradition of heathen sanctity. According to legend, this first mission met with gross incivility, which was ribald and rough rather than violent, and the Saint resorted to a magic of his own to overcome the old powers. Thereafter Heil, as an eleventh-century chronicler tells us he was called by the pagan Saxons, shared the valley with another God, whose neophytes purified the waters that had long been sacred. Later, an abbey was raised on the spot. Now, only the Abbot's gateway remains, opening onto a field at the foot of Giant Hill where masses of Poole oyster shells are still to be found under mounds on the site of the Abbot's kitchen.

Many writers comment with amazement on the tolerance shown by church and abbey in allowing the Giant, 'with such indecent circumstances as to make one conclude it was also a Priapus', to remain intact; for this survival depends upon active participation in his scouring, once undertaken by villagers and Black Friars, and now by the Ministry of Works. Some believe that he was maintained as an image of the vanquished, with the Conqueror's seal scored between his legs: Jehovah Hoc Destruxit. It is possible, I suppose, and equally possible that his maintenance represented much the same impulse that led to the foundation of churches inside ancient circles. In Britain the greatest stone circle, Stonehenge, was known as the Giant's Dance; it has been pointed out, in connection with the Giant of Cerne, that there is a Hele stone at Stonehenge. It is clear that Helith was also, apart from his more occult apsects, what Professor Stuart Piggott has called Hercules, 'peculiarly a god of the common people'. I like to think that this had something to do with his survival.

SOLENT SHORE

NEW YEAR'S DAY AT LEPE

Set out on a morning of white thaw
smoking between oaks, Hatchet Pond so still
it might have been frozen
except for the long slender rods
as if painted on its dark blue glaze.
Saw nothing of the *Private, Keep Out*
notices of semi-feudal estates,
but cock pheasants in brown fields
of sharp-edged clods, poking out their necks.
Then the small rusty bell of the shingle
tinkled and grated as it dragged,
a shadowy tanker bared its round stern
and Marchwood power station exhaled
a breath which the sun tinged pink;
but of all things none seemed newer
than gravel with its sheen of fresh oranges
at the water's lip. Brought away that,
and an old transparent moon
over the Island, the delicate industrial sky
blue-grey as a herring gull's back,
and a small sunny boy running beside
the great wet novelty shouting *wasser, wasser.*

PAINTINGS

for my father

Avon weir pouring

suspended, the race
brushed still, river
and sky, shadow,
sunlight and trees rushing

enclosed, opening
the house on water.

Slow Boldre,
slower Stour:
gold shallows;
dark, Forest pools

or where they run
dammed—white whorl
of an eddy, or flow
barred—green, brown

pass from seclusion
of leaf and earth,
blue oils spreading
contained:

Christchurch fluid
on the wall,
the shore at Keyhaven
where an easel stood.

SHINGLE SPIT

Where the next moment
wiped out the last impression
the sea had raised
a wall of shingle.
Slippery reefs of kelp
blotched the water; sandbars
barely covered, shone like bullion.
The Island showed plainly
what it was: the splintered foot
of a bridge, and on a surface
hacked into crests
the chalk blue waves reflected it.
They broke, of course,
and a slow, dark pulse
beat rhythmically in the sand.
It will not be like that now,
and was not then.
I expected to hold nothing visible,
and did not, though my steps
remade a pattern they had long become.

RAT ISLAND

1
With first light
The bearings surface.

From Tennyson's memorial
To Sway tower,
From Jack in the basket
To Fawley,
Point after point
Rises on time.

I mark them,
Borne back
On a freshening wind.

The sea completes the circle.

   2
There are no rats;
Except at high spring,
No island.

Only a relic
Of the late defences
Harbouring
Mud-dwellers.

Part of the shore
That curves away,
Keen as a tern's wing.

   3
I have stayed long enough
Casting a shadow.

     Let it be
As it is
When a tern dives
And on the blue sky
In the water, between
The smooth hulls
Of mudbanks,
The wind casts waving lines.

PITTS DEEP

Over Abbey ploughland
On a brown, winter day
Of Cistercian calm,

No one will go observing
The silver bell mouth of the sky,
Or cross the manorial path
Into oakwoods descending
Almost to the water—
Except, perhaps, two friends
With a bottle of cheap wine
Who walk in confessional mood
Where forest ponies also go,
Trampling soiled, silky weed
On mudbanks and quills
Of bleached salt-grass,
Sowing a trail of droppings
On the stilled shore.

FRIEND WITH A MANDOLIN

Singer with a mandolin,
Pluck from the smoke
Of a humdrum bar
The raw defiant strings
Of Mountjoy and Van Diemen's Land,

Let the bland south
Hear the blues.

From the cradle
Twanging in your hands,
Pick Café Mozart.

At closing time, we'll sit out
On the shingle drunkenly
Amazed to think of France,
So far away, still serving wine.

WEST WIGHT

Was it idolatry or love?

Nettles hide the sign.
Through the heart
of this deep green hollow
the road leads on.

Then on the high domed crown
thyme and all grass end
gulls shriek below
nothing to lean on but the wind.

Do not ask me to take you there,
no, not for a phial of coloured sand.

Stand with me here on the shore,
watching the white island,
stark as a statue, fall into mist.

Turn back with me, always
turn back, my love.

BY SOUTHAMPTON WATER

The water is bottle green, with a salt crust
And an unmistakable flavour of sewage.

A tarred gull floats past; an orange box
And the helmet of a marine; a glove
With the hand still in it.

Going home,
The view from Totton flyover
Makes me gape
Even now.
    The river's wedge broadens
Seaward; a dream of cranes swims in haze;
Smoke from the power station silvers the blue.
Everywhere, men I know work under it.
Necessities are unladen and shipped.
That is the root.

Black ribs of a hull in the mud.
'It's a Viking,' my parents said.

'Viking': the word's skeleton of spars
With sky through it,
Sticking up from blue-grey mud.

As the song goes:
    When the tide is out at Totton
    The stench is something rotten . . .

True; but I cannot imagine sea without it;
Without gumboot-sucking ooze;
Small green crabs sidling by old green posts;
Without tugs and the giant Queens.

At night, crossing to Hythe,
The water squirms with ideograms.

I could spare a life trying to decipher them.

THE WATER'S EDGE

In a time between
flying boat and hovercraft,
between stained tanks
through villages, and waves
of Solent City:

in a place over
caved-in paths echoing
the tidal swill,
over windrows of shell
and beaker: here

I return, like sun
on the river's green back
that cannot pierce it,
or remain, like stones
I once threw, working
a blind passage in the mud.

Though waves set hard
along the coast,
and new amphibians
displace the old,
part of me stays
at the water's edge,
greased with use, among
corks, tarred feathers,
bits of boats, tins
knocking against the wall.

SOLENT WINTER

1

Yachts on the leaden estuaries
are wingless, larval.
Leeward of the island
rusty bums of tankers
squat in the swell.
This full-bodied water
bears its trademark in oil.

Now the tides grease a shore
stripped to its working parts.
High over the cranes
Fawley Beacon burns.

2

On short dim evenings
the grey island floats off-shore
like a ghostly berg;
liners are lit up for Christmas
with the stores.

Where Southampton Water forks
the town is grounded
on gravel shoals.
Funnels converge on the centre.
Portholes and windows shine.
The streets trap echoes
of muted horns.

Wires still buzz with messages
from the *Titanic*.
A seance breaks up
when a cabin-boy screams.

ON A PHOTOGRAPH OF SOUTHAMPTON DOCKS

for Brian Maidment

Blinding silver on grey,
a suntrack points deep
into this average morning.
All is ready for work:
launches at their moorings,
small tubs off the pierhead,
warehouses; and above all
the cranes, these flying high
or with pulleys dangling,
those far back, more spidery.
No, it is not their function
to please the eye.
Yet they do—more so
for the common goodness
of their function, for grace
extra to a working world
that neighbours sky and water,
drawing from all
some ordinary tribute;
for that reason too,
more beautiful, as they say:
like birds, like dancers.

ON SPEDE'S MAP ANNO DOMINI 1611

Four craft ride light
off West Key, two
by the Water Gate,
an easterly fills the sails
of a merchantman.
Castle and churches stand out
inside the walls,
houses press together
in the form of hieroglyphs.

On Gods house grene
two citizens play at bowls
with a watchman.
Empty, the streets appear
neither plagued nor decaying.
Waves crawl in
like water snakes, or eyebrows
raised—a child's gulls.
Halted at rush hour
on the roof of a carpark,
smoky cloud hailing
where the sea was, on acres
of containers, the image
reappears—unreadable
except by one for whom
the sky not on the map
existed quite ordinarily.

HOLY ROOD

Below Bar, through the gate
That is always open,
Many made the passage
Grief makes back.

Only the great anchor
In the bombed church
Will not drag.

Its fluke in the nave
Holds all who pass
To brief observance,

But leaves a centre
That is always fixed
Where all stream through.

CANUTE ROAD

'Go back,' he says,
knowing it won't,
the long tide standing.
Yet it does, over and over again,
greening gravel with weed,
and leaving now and then
a hand-axe or faceless coin.
Image passes into image,
name under name, down the road
between medieval gatehouse
and docks, that ends with a cold smell
where the floating bridge runs out
and shipyards dominate the shore.

FROM A PILL-BOX ON THE SOLENT

On a day of ripped cloud,
Angled light, wind against tide,
I am tempted to begin
The story of my life.

Waves come from far off,
Through the gap they have made,
Between Purbeck and Wight.

Surf booms in the pill-box,
Rattles the shingle,
Folds over it, unfolds,
Laying it bare.

Let it blow sand or salt.
Here at least I tread without fear
Of unsettling dust.

SOLENT SHORE

Where the shoreline ends
At the horizon, the far sky's
Pronged with orange flames
From the refinery.

Today the clouds bear east,
Forming a broad, shadowy space
Of dark green mudlands,
Staked out with old stumps,
With rows of masts along
Estuaries and creeks.

It might be almost any time,
As one slow hulk of cloud
Lags to the west, mirrored
Like an oil slick off the Needles.

RICE GRASS
(*Spartina Townsendii*)

Praise one appearing
lowly, no man's rose,
but with roots far-reaching
out and down.

Give homage to a spartan cross,
native and American,
hardier and more adaptable
than those; nearly a newcomer
but one that, by staying put
has made itself a home;
also a traveller east and west.

Celebrate the entertainer
of sea aster, sea lavender,
thrift and nesting gulls;
lover of mud and salt;
commoner and useful colonist,
converter from ooze
of land where a foot may fall.

THE WITNESSES

1 *Salterns*

The late King of blessed memory,
by his letters patent,
dated 14th July
in the fourth year of his reign,
for a great debt and faithful service
done by Robert Pamplyn, Esq
to Queen Elizabeth, King James,
and his late majesty
did grant to Dame Mary,
widow of Sir George Wandesford,
and Margaret his sister,
daughters and co-heirs
of the said Robert Pamplyn,
certain Marish and Ouzy Lands,
usually over-flowen by the sea,
within the County of Southampton;
rendering rent to the King,
fourpence per acre when gained . . .

Yeoman of the Robes
to three monarchs—an estate of mud!

Salt, of course: remarkably
fine and white—

at Oxey of the Dutchmen,
or Newfoundland
(which they made possible)
or Normandy,
named after Cobbett's farm
by a radical.
(Cobbett, who admired
the hog rubbing his shoulders
against a column—font
and holy water gone—
from Beaulieu: *fine place*
he explained in homely terms
to his host; admired
the order of monks no less,
and the view: one of the finest
that ever was seen in the world;
found farmer John Biel
hospitable, and, there,
no skin and bone and nakedness.)

A cloud of steam filled
the boiling-house;
salt impregnated the air;
roads all around were
black with coal-ashes
from the furnaces,
generation after generation
incessantly burning . . .

Great debt, faithful service, yet
however fine and white, the salt
could not preserve its use
against the steam-engine.

Salterns: Normandy Lane
leads to Oxey
generation after generation.
Still everywhere

the regular channels
and embankments,
lagoons deployed for leisure;
the savour:
hints of an Old Master.
Beyond marish and ouzy land,
silver, the open passage

2 Mary Rose (1545)

Sunk by her own guns
cannoning to leeward,
gunports open to the sea.

The King he screeched
like any maid:
'Oh my gentlemen.
Oh my gallent men.'

All over. The cry of mun,
the screech of mun, Oh Sir,
up to the very heavens.

The very last souls I seen
was that man's father
and that man's.

Drowned like rattens,
drowned like rattens.

3 In a manner enduring

1
In a manner dying
    with age, but—

Tide's coming up!
    bears wine
cleare & white hued,
faire orient red.

Not always must a man
close his eyes
clench his teeth
filter the stuff
wry mouthed & shuddering.

Not at Clausentum
for patrons of Ancasta.

Not at Suthamtun.

Or over undercrofts
built on tuns of wine,
woolsacks, woolfells.
    Agnus Dei.

No other men than
gilded merchants,
no other world but England.

   2
Tide's coming up!
    bears ever
a floating population,
carrack & galley, wherry & cog.

Long oarsmen
of Hamwic, Wulfheard's kin,
graves dug through graves
under the gasworks.

Confluent founders,
incendiaries: Francons;

Fleming burgesses;
Latin tenders
　　of goods and names.

Dalmatian oarsmen,
patrons of St Nicholas,
sharing a grave.

Men of Northam
boasting of Alfred.
Men of Itchen
boasting of Olaf.

　　Floating,
　　ever-rolling,

their oars drip silver.

　3
It's a long haul
from the Watergate, or Bargate.
For Cambridge, Gray and Scrope
the wind sets foul.

　　A long haul
for the poor naked foot.
For musters; regiments
with limbers, horses, mules.
For men and women
　　of Area C.

　　Undercrofts
shelter them, or they trudge
with prams and pushcarts;
wander the woods
　　till morning.

Between booms,
after epidemics,
      in a manner dying.

Not always must a man
doctoring the poor
die of his vocation.

All the same for them.
Where can we go?
      We have complained
till we are tired.

      Dying
over curative waters;
docks from mudlands;
arrivals, departures.
      Enduring
our continual stream
to the land of gold.

TIDE-RACE

High water: the sea asleep
In oily ripples, rocking
A bleared, whole sun.
Then the tide begins to turn,
Gathering speed, bores
Tunnels through wrack,
Ploughs deep furrows
Through a shingle blizzard.
Where bass may keep their heads
A six-ounce lead trips away,
Dancing over ledges; the fisherman,
Woken by a shrieking ratchet,
Is hooked for an instant fast

In the running sea, before
His line flies loose. Drumming
Under his feet, cresting where
It brushes a shoal, shouldering
The adjacent slack into ridges,
The broad channel races through,
White sparks flying from its back.

WHERE THE GRAVEL SHELVES

From the shallows of sleep,
Out where the gravel shelves,
The sharp white rocks passing,
The shore, the open sea, passing,
Taller the white rocks,
Farther the shore, closer
But less attainable
The open sea . . .
You, chin above water,
Always afraid of the undertow,
The firm foot slipping, you
Whose strongest emotion was fear
Approach now the dreamless, deep
Stillness, silent as a ship's bell
Stopped with a bell of mud.

GRACEDIEU (1418-)

No ungodly siege,
no maiden voyage.

Her unwritten log
a stroke of lightning,
decay near the key

from which she sailed
upstream,
to a mud berth.

Her good timber made
roofs shipshape.
Her rotten beams breed
untrue histories.

Ghost of a Viking.

Shadowy virgin
gracing the silt.

PROSPECT OF BOLDRE CHURCH

Raised above oaks
Above a full river.

Once the living
Of William Gilpin.
Now his quiet mansion.

He hopes to rise
In God's good time.

Dim, coloured light
Stains the sanctuary,
The lettered stones
Charged with patience.

Things that seem misplaced
Catch the eye
Irresistibly,
Even as it bends:

H.M.S. Hood;
The Book of Remembrance,
Names illuminated
Of the able-bodied.

The head inclined to bow
Remains unshocked,
But cold; observes

St Nicholas
Overlooking benches
Carved with her crest;
Pictures the sea

Outside the frame: colder
For fires quenched in a flash,
For steel made a harrow
Useless on the ocean bed;

Even here, enclosed
Above oaks above
A full river, the sea
Open, spirited shipless.

AT OSBORNE HOUSE

Under cedar and ilex,
On lawns to us *verboten*,
Convalescents watch us,
From coach and car,
Mobbing their repose.

            His too,
Albert of Saxe-Coburg's,
His bay of Naples, his
Renaissance villa,

His evergreens, which,
After more than a century,
Cast longer and darker shadows.

If it were quiet, if
I could attend,
I might imagine
Innumerable salutes,
            the waterway
Busy with despatches,
Screwed and churning,
Hatched with white, cross lines.

Among her many possessions
The Empress of grief
Becomes her statue,
            marble
Among marble and horn,
Silver and ivory, mahogany and teak.

Here is India, here
St Petersburg
On a vase of Nicholas I,
Here Kaiser Wilhelm
Of the waxed aspiring moustache.
            The musical-box
Plays a march from *Tannhaüser*.

She is Britannia;
To her Neptune entrusts
The Command of the Sea.

The finish is perfect,
A spectacle,
Complete—
Like the royal children's marble limbs.

I would rather look out,
Down terraces of statuary,

Over woods of oak and beech,
Elms dying or dead,
To the blue Solent,
Spithead,
The tower blocks of Portsmouth.

The young Queen bathing
For the first time
Ducked her head:
'I thought I should be stifled.'

On the balcony with Albert
She heard the nightingales.
Here, by royal decree
The past tense shall prevail.

AT THE STATUE OF ISAAC WATTS

1
Image set
Among sticky buds:

Dated, the marble
Establishes a prodigal
Home for good.

Clear through traffic,
Trains and horns
The Civic Centre chimes
'Our God, our help . . .'

2
The measured tide
Moves congregations;
Its undertow sways
Outside the walls.

Across the narrow sea
From Western Shore
(Refinery hazy
Under the Forest)
An impure land delights.

Against sluggard wit
And muddy spirit,
Dr Watts stands proof.

At his granite base,
Place tributary strands
Of living wrack.

POSTSCRIPT

(i.m. V.)

Alive, no
doubt of that, no
doubt when shingle
kicks my ankle bone

And lightning splits
my clouded mind

A Baez song:
sweet voice through
fall of hair

        black hair
        long fingers
picking a guitar
        long fingers
picked

And lightning—
        daggers

twisted   scattered
silver points

A tall lithe figure
                              races
up the shelving spit
between the mud-banked estuary
& sea

I lag behind
                              Or
Floating pools
on pools,
a mirage
icy blue, dark blue

Stopped wordless
till the stones grew cold
when hand in hand . . .

Those letters now
(if kept)
are monologues
                              were
monologues

(You said
I never saw you
'As I am')

Love, then, for love
of eloquence?

A fever shook my hand
that held the pen

All that—but under all
our friendship
nothing now can hide

My dear—

Enclosed: some sea pink
& a pinch of thyme

YAFFLE

The last of ebb:
Silver eeling in creeks,
Dinghies on their sides,
Cracked mudflats:

Palm, veins branching,
From which I walk.

Over deep falls,
Smelling leafmould,
Brine and dead crab,
I hear the echo
Of a laughing yaffle.

Who cares who comes
Who goes? pecker, green

Don't-give-a damn
Woodpecker. Circling
Unseen, he laughs, drums,
Rounds all I see.

The silver between oaks
Is a ring
Gathering friends.

Deeper the echoes fathom
Sounding dugouts,

Stumps of a forest
Under peat under sea.

From woods I turn
To an estuary flooded,
Reflecting branches,
Gulls frosty against
A pale, full moon.

BIRTH

I held your mother, child.
She was beyond me.

The shout forced from deep inside
Came shrill: shout
Of a body hurt and labouring
To an end: of a self lost,
Willing unwilled, giving
Delivered.
           I was not afraid
Though a storm's blue light
Flickered on steel, made the room
Tropical, dangerous.
One of the masked attendants,
I held her, beyond myself.

Hair more like seaweed on a stone
Stuck to the crown; then
A creased and slippery form
Came in a gush of blood,
More naked
Than a mussel eased from its shell,
Stranger, more ancient,
Than a creature long-drowned.

Breath came with a cry,
Earthly unearthly cry.
The knot was cut, and tied.

Outside, I watched rain drip
From railings of a balcony,
Form pools on the roof below.

Still on my wrist I feel
The reddish fluid
Where the waters breaking fell.

GULL ON A POST

Gull on a post firm
In the tideway—how I desire
The gifts of both!

Desire against the diktat
Of intellect: be single,
You who are neither.

As the useful one
That marks a channel, marks
Degrees of neap and spring;
Apt to bear jetties
Or serve as a mooring;
Common, staked with its like.

Standing ever
Still in one place,
It has a look of permanence.

Riddled with shipworm,
Bored by the gribble,
In a few years it rots.

Desire which tears at the body
Would fly unconstrained
Inland or seaward; settle
At will—but voicing
Always in her cry
Essence of wind and wave,
Bringing to city, moorish
Pool and ploughland,
Reminders of storm and sea.

Those who likened the soul
To a bird, did they ever
Catch the eye of a gull?

Driven to snatch,
Fight for slops in our wake.

Or voice a desolation
Not meant for us,
Not even desolate,
But which we christen.

Folk accustomed to sin,
Violent, significant death,
Who saw even in harbour
Signs terrible and just,
Heard in their cries
Lost souls of the drowned.

Gull stands on a post
In the tideway; I see

No resolution; only
The necessity of flight
Beyond me, firm
Standing only then.

UNDER MYNYDD BACH

WINTER PRELUDE

A magpie out of Breughel
Draws his long, straight tail
Across the cold still-life;
The naked stream runs black
Below the barely parted
Overhangs of snow.
No human voice or chirrup
Where the night fall rests.

A new year, and a snowfall
Hardly marked—still
The unbelieving self is still.
I look from emptiness
Towards the covering snow.

Wales, I find below
Your silence and your sound
A silence harder than the rock
To break and deeper than the snow.

BEIDOG

Sunlight and shallow water,
rock, stones with red marks
like cuts of a rusty axe,
dark under hazel and alder,
broken white on blackened steps
and below the falls a cold pale green—

how shall I celebrate this,
    always present
under our sleep and thoughts,
where we do not see ourselves
    reflected
or know the language of memory
gathered from its fall?

Beidog running dark
    between us
and our neighbours, down
from Mynydd Bach—
this is the stream I wish to praise
    and the small mountain.

I am not of you, tongue
through whom Taliesin descends the ages
gifted with praise, who know
that praise turns dust to light.
    In my tongue,
of all arts
this is the most difficult.

SOFT DAYS AFTER SNOW

Soft days after snow,
    snowdrops
under sycamores beside the stream,
earth brown and crumbling.

Now the dark gleams softly
under catkins and water below,
alight in the February sun.
And I who desired
    eyes washed clean
as melting snow,

radiant at the point of fall,
know that every word obscures
the one I want to know.

Now soft days bear us
who take each other's hands,
and on their surface
    colder than blood
our brief appearances.

Though snowdrops follow the snow,
    and the water burns,
darkness carries them.

Our faces are taken away.

Where do you go,
    unspeakable love?

ON SAINT DAVID'S DAY

For Dewi Sant, an eye
of yellow in the daffodils,
the curlew from the sea,
the hare that lollops by a gate
    which opens wide
on far Plynlimmon,
Cader Idris
and the airy rockface
    of the northern sky.

I too would name
a tribute of these things:
cold wind,
white sun of March,
    the boundaries

whose handywork of stone
shines through the falling earth.

I turn towards the mynydd
in a film of light,
    and turning
ask of Dewi Sant
    his benediction
on these words that settle
where the uplands rise.

CURLEW

The curve of its cry—
A sculpture
Of the long beak:
A spiral carved from bone.

It is raised
    quickening
From the ground,
Is wound high, and again unwound,
    down
To the stalker nodding
In a marshy field.

It is the welling
Of a cold mineral spring,
Salt from the estuary
Dissolved, sharpening
The fresh vein bubbling on stone.

It is an echo
Repeating an echo
That calls you back.

It looses
Words from dust till the live tongue
Cry: This is mine
Not mine, this life
Welling from springs
Under ground, spiralling
Up the long flight of bone.

THE MASON'S LAW

Though the slate
where his hand slipped
could not stand
    worthy of a name,
at least it could lie
in his living room,
set in the floor.

Er Cof unfinished,
under our feet, recalls
the mason and his law:
    Honour the dead
with your craft;
waste nothing; leave
no botched memorial.

BRYNBEIDOG

For ten years the sycamores
have turned about us, the Beidog
has run with leaves, and ice and sun.
I have turned the earth, thrown up
blue chip and horseshoe; from near fields
sheep and bullocks have looked in.

We have shared weathers
with the stone house; kept its silence;
listened under winds lifting slates
for a child's cry; all we have
the given space has shaped, pointing
our lights seen far off
as a spark among scattered sparks.
   The mountain above
has been rock to my drifting mind.

Where all is familiar, around us
the country with its language
gives all things other names;
there is darkness on bright days
and on the stillest a wind
that will not let us settle,
but blows the dust from loved
things not possessed or known.

WIND BLEW ONCE

Wind blew once till it seemed
the earth would be skinned from the fields,
the hard roots bared.
   Then it was again
a quiet October,
red berries on grey rock
and blue sky, with a buzzard crying.

I scythed half-moons in long grass,
with nettle-burn stinging my arms,
bringing the blood's rhythm back.
   At night
in our room we lay in an angle
between two streams,
with sounds of water meeting,

and by day
the roads ran farther,
joined and formed a pattern
at the edge of vast, cloudy hills.

The house was small
against the mountain; from above,
a stone on a steep broad step
of falling fields; but around us
the walls formed a deep channel,
with marks of other lives, holding
its way from worked moorland
to this Autumn with an open sky.

COMMON LAND ABOVE TREFENTER

This is no haunt
For the painter of prospects.

Sheep will not bleat a complaint
Or the barn owl hoot derision,
Where poverty abounded
Providing shelter.

On bared common, where
Nocturnal migrants homed,
There is room for the kite
Cleaned out of cities, none
For the import of terror,

For alien shadow
In common daylight,
Or fashion
Of nightmare or grandeur:

Thin cawl
On the valley's bread line
Is not its provider, nor
Dwellings built in a night,
Fields wide as an axe throw
From the door, patterning
Moorland with stony patches.

Only the bare history
Under foot—holdings

Untenable, falling back
Into quarries: last post
Of hedge-bank craftsmen,
With breast plough and mattock,
On the road to the coalface.

HILL COUNTRY RHYTHMS

for Robert Wells

Sometimes I glimpse a rhythm
I am not part of, and those who are
could never see.
    The hawk I disturb
at his kill, leaving bodiless,
bloody wings spread, curves
away and with a sharp turn
follows the fence; and the fence
lining a rounded bank flies
smoothly downhill, then rises
to wind-bowed trees whose shape
the clouds take on, and the ridge
running under them, where
the sky bears round in a curve.
On the mountainside stands
a square white farm, its roof
a cutting edge, but it too

moves with shadow and cloud.
    I glimpse this
with the hawk in view, lose it
to fenceposts and trees holding
a still day down, and wings
dismembered at my feet, while
down the road comes a neighbour
singing loudly, with his herd
big-uddered, slowly swaying.

AS A THOUSAND YEARS

Not a soul, only
a stubble field, bales
like megaliths; a flight
of trees over the Beidog,
and behind, darker green,
at the back of the sky,
the ridge damming
the sun; then,
    for a breath,
there was no sign of us.
Not a soul, only
light flooding this field
bright as a marigold.

REVIVAL, 1904

They hung on the word.

It does not matter
the slopes of Hafod Ithel
are empty now; empty
as their farms that summer.

Judgement is the rockface.

It does not matter
you will hear no echo
of prayer or praise
across Llyn Eiddwen's water.

They were crossed with light.

A NEIGHBOUR

I remembered his laugh—once
he almost fell from a chair;
also with one hammerblow
he drove a fencepost in.
Some weeks I saw only him,
with his dogs and stick, old coat
and greasy cap, walking
from the mountain to his fields;
and we talked—we said aye
to everything, with a language
between us, and rare china
civility, out in wind, rain or sun.
He was first to welcome us,
standing in the door saying aye, aye . . .

I would have seen him then,
strangely white, thinning the hedge
with a hook, his old coat hung on a branch;
but instead a flock of starlings
turned me aside—a swirl
of black flecks over the valley.
Then, seeing the graveyard,
I did not look again
at the hedge, with white, jagged ends.

SHEPHERD

Others have died or left;
he has grown louder, bigger,
filling the fields which he keeps
with an old skill.

I picture him through glass,
framed in the window,
against the mountain:

tall, strongly made,
ruddy from wind and sun,
a man who strides, sings,
waves a stick, then shouts
at his dogs with a voice
they will hear in the village.

And he turns, walks
through the frame, as he has
since he came as a boy
and stood with his father
saying aye, aye . . .

PWYLL THE OLD GOD

> 'I would be glad to see a wonder,' said Pwyll
> 'I will go and sit on the hill.'
>
> *The Mabinogion*

Pwyll the old god
may look through you,
when you look through eyes
of spiderwebs, through
tiny rainbows brilliant
as bluebottle shards, and see,

in a dance of gold flecks,
the mountain hang by a strand.

This may be his emblem:
a ram's skull with a thread
of silk between its horns,
but certainly you see
the everyday, the wonder:

Old windblown light
fresh as this morning;
rooks with black breasts
and silver backs; clear-cut
shadows brightening fields,
and over the ridge the sun,
curve of a dark body
in blinding white; everywhere
fragments of web shining,
that look like ends.

EMILY

The season is late; our long shadow
with two clothes peg heads notched
one above the other lies flat across the field;
and from above me, breaking
the quiet of sleepy baas and caws,
an excited voice exclaims
at a sudden vision:
    a yellow digger
uprooting bushes, changing the stream's
meanders to a straighter course.

Now our single track divides,
a dark fork in dew-grey grass,
and a small girl in a red frock,

sun yellowing her fair hair, runs
away from me with a bunch
of corn marigolds, campion,
harebells and a magpie feather
crushed in her fist.

Away she runs through a drift
of thistledown, seeds
stuck to her bare wet legs;
runs away laughing, shouting
for me to catch her—
but I know now that I never will;
   never, my darling,
but run with care, run lightly
with the light about you,
run to the gate through moist soft grass,
webs and bright blades all about you,
   hint of a rainbow
in the silver shower at your heels.

LINES TO A BROTHER

to Tony Hooker

Waking early today,
I think of you preparing
for work, driving through
a quiet Oxfordshire dawn.

   You will join
sawn timbers, intimate
as their owners will never be
with roof-tree and joist,
while I lie awake, watching
light form the bulk of Mynydd Bach.

   I see your hands,
steadied by the recreation

of labour, and again
the morning air tastes thin;
   once more I turn
to images of the skilled life
we have drawn from and shared,
in whose absence
my words offer no habitation.

BEHIND THE LIGHTS

Last night, I looked from the Island.
   Then I was again
behind the lights, living there
blindly, where the mainland
long shore shone, with breaks
at Forest and river mouths,
a ghostly smoke round chimneys;
till suddenly, a green light
on black water cut across my view.

Tonight, I return
to another darkness, the house
strangely cold, behind me
the long road back to Wales.
It will be dark in an hour
but now the sun setting
picks out a fox in the field
above the house, cutting across my view.
There he goes gingerly,
a lordly fox, golden red.
   Tired, I see
a green light on black water.
Better to follow the fox,
from sunlight into shadow,
on his cold way home.

PRAYER IN JANUARY

Now when the old New Year
Starts red with sun on snow,
Must resolution splinter
Like a frosted bough?
The stars of ancient January
Hurt the eyes; by day, like stars,
Snow crystals make them ache.
But Yahweh's eyes burn clear
As drops that fall from alders
By the mountain stream.
They are not stars or melting snow
But outstare every star
And every thing most star-like
In this old, cold, flaming universe.

Soft heart, small, bitter pool
Beneath your darkening hemisphere
Of ice, hidden eyes blaze
Where you hide. Regard
Their hard regard, that weighs
The worth of all you guard
At not a fraction of its price.
Let love outlast such love
As self, too tender of itself,
Has dreamed regardless of a sight
More pitiless, more pitiful than you.
Then be unselved, or drying
When the eyes burn through
Die dreamless into hard-ribbed clay.

SYCAMORE BUDS

Then speak, not
from the shell of self,
its beaten walls, but
as these pointed buds
with tight, green scales
the winter could not loose
and waste the rising force
erecting spikes, that
lengthen, curving
into soft, closed beaks
that open on their tongues
and now unfold small hands:
wrinkled, blood-red leaves,
fresh and glistening
damp—shapes of the force
they are, containing them.

DRAGONS IN THE SNOW

Thaw to the hedgerows
left white crosses on the hill,
     the first thrush sang.

Now a buzzard cries, confirming
     silence under all.

The few bare trees are darker
for the fall that covers
     boundaries,
and in their place reveals
contrasting absolutes.

We are so small,
the boy and I, between
the snowclouds and the snow.

He starts from here,
who talks of dragons
as we walk, the first today
to leave a human sign
beside the marks of sheep and crow.

He warms me
with confiding hand
and fiery talk,
   who also start
upon the ground
of choice, the silence
answering the choice;
happy to be small, and walk,
and hear of dragons in the snow.

AFTERWORD

This summer, I have completed a critical book, *Poetry of Place*, consisting of essays and reviews written during the period 1969-1980, and made a selection from my own four books of poems. With this work done, the present naturally feels to me like a time of uncertain transition between phases or movements in my life and writing, and in consequence the invitation* to write about my work offers me a greater than usual temptation to be retrospectively wise. But of course, the feeling must be distrusted. For every sequence, every poem even, is a new beginning, which yet relates in some way to what has gone before. All the same, there are other reasons, too, which support my feeling that with these books at least part of a movement—and of course, I hope it is only part!—may be seen. I will try to sketch it here.

By the time this essay appears, we shall probably not still be living in the place—Brynbeidog, Llangwyryfon—in which I am writing it, which is the centre of *Englishman's Road* and the place where, looking out on Welsh uplands, I have written most of my poems set in the south of England. I owe no place more than Llangwyryfon, but it has taken eleven years of living there, in an agricultural and predominantly Welsh-speaking community, for us to realise that our particular kind of dislocation can't be mended by settling permanently where other people belong.

It was in this house that I wrote, mostly during the summer when our son was born, *Soliloquies of a Chalk Giant*. This was my first published book of poems, though written after the completion of *Landscape of the Daylight Moon*, which was published third. As I have written elsewhere, in words that apply to all my poetry, my aim in

*The invitation came from Dr John Rowlands, editor of *Llais Llyfrau*. I reprint the essay here, with some slight revision, to mark my sense of the movement which these poems, together with the book of critical essays, represent.

Soliloquies 'was not to make a prepared statement, but to
explore all that the image (of the Cerne giant) contained'. I
give primacy to my subject matter or materials, with an
exploratory, attentive approach to it, to see what it has to
say. I do this not from any doctrine of impersonality but
in accordance with the principle so succinctly expressed by
David Jones in his Preface to *The Anathemata*: 'one is
trying to make a shape out of the very things of which one
is oneself made'. This I associate with another quotation
which is for me a touchstone, and indicates how impossible
it would be for 'the very things of which one is oneself
made' to be either merely private or confined to one's
lifetime. This is Waldo Williams's

> Beth yw gwladgarwch? Cadw ty
> Mewn cwmwl tystion.
>
> [What is love of country? Keeping house
> Amid a cloud of witnesses.]

    The chalk giant sequence was part of a continuing
movement, precipitated and strongly affected by my
living in Wales, in which I have come to see and feel my
original home ground in the south of England as I could
never have done had I stayed there. And as I might not
have done had I gone to some area where the sense of
cydymdreiddiad is felt less strongly—but I'm not sure, for
although I am unfortunately unable to read the Welsh
philosopher J. R. Jones in the original, I suspect from
what I have read of this idea of his, that I would have
experienced its truth in any circumstances. For example,
when I read in Ned Thomas's recent study of Derek
Walcott his description of *cydymdreiddiad* as 'that subtle
knot of interpenetration, which . . . grows in time (in
people's consciousness) between a territory and its people
and their language, creating a sense of belonging to a parti-
cular stretch of the earth's surface', I felt that this is what
I sensed blindly as a child, and have for years been struggling
to express, in an unphilosophical way. I have two further

touchstones for 'the very things', and brevity may allow me to juxtapose them suggestively, though it would require a book to draw out their implications and connections. One is Edward Thomas's poem 'Words', especially his description of words as

> dear
> As the earth which you prove
> That we love.

The other is from Thomas Traherne's *Centuries*:

> Some things are little on the outside, and rough and common, but I remember the time when the dust of the streets were as precious as Gold to my infant eyes, and now they are more precious to the eye of reason.

The movement began with my 'first' book, *Landscape of the Daylight Moon*, and continued through *Solent Shore* into *Englishman's Road*, the heart of which is set in Wales, 'under Mynydd Bach' in the hill country south east of Aberystwyth. In previous collections I had, by a sleight of imagination, as it were, written as if from immediately within southern England, as firmly rooted there as an old post in Southampton Water. It is in fact my conviction that English poetry, wherever it is written geographically, most needs, for its revitalisation, to be written not from 'above' or 'outside'—from a position of ironical self-conscious detachment, for example—but from *inside* a world which the poet shares with others, living and dead: a world in time and place, subject to all the influences that shape a specific human identity. An irony of which I am painfully aware is that distance from my place has sharpened my sense of it, and made my poems of Southampton, for example, not what I wish they were, a citizen's, but an exile's. At the same time, the value I find in differences between people and places has been increased by my experience of Wales as a foreigner, in a position that allows me as an Englishman neither confidence nor complacency. My sympathy with some Anglo-Welsh poets arises not only because they are friends, but because their sense of place seems born of an unease similar to mine, which comes from being an outsider on the inside. As a critic and teacher, I am totally opposed to those institutions and the consciousness they breed, which would make all but their own people feel 'outside'—outside London, or Oxbridge, or, it may be, Cardiff or Aberystwyth. . . . A poetry that sets things in place, affirms that sense of each place being its own 'centre' which is still far commoner than the official centres would have us believe, but is now in desperate need of the artist's fidelity to his witnesses and things.

I spoke earlier of my belief in the primacy of subject matter or materials. My word for this is 'ground', by which I mean, briefly, a total environment, human and non-human, historical and personal, experienced through every form of relevant knowledge available to one, yet known as directly as the shock through one's whole body of treading on a stone, and through a language that was learnt there, in relation to the world it composes. It follows from this that it would take me some years of living in Wales before I could write of this 'ground' with conviction, and that in writing of Wales in English I should be acutely aware of tensions between my language and subject, and between my Englishness and the Welshness of the place. Certainly there have been, and are, tensions. But also, in writing the 'Under Mynydd Bach' sequence of *Englishman's Road*, I felt myself an explorer, and one who was 'translating' the things of a particular area of Wales into an alien tongue for the first time. I experienced all the conflicts implicit in that act. I felt my relation to those three English 'intruders' on Mynydd Bach that were the subject of a typescript study by Dr Richard Phillips, from which I learnt the details of Augustus Brackenbury's intrusion in the 1820s—subject of the radio poem which gives its title to the book. I myself was in some ways an enemy of the very place I had come to love, yet I felt at times something of the newness and wonder of the day when Adam named the creatures. In this place with its native language, every thing had an otherness which I wanted to name and honour in my own tongue, yet of which I could not make a shape without helping to dishonour, perhaps. . . . In any case, I came at last to a point beyond which there were only three possibilities, none of which I could accept: assimilation, as far as possible, into Welsh-speaking Wales; expression of isolation within this community; or further tension between my English words and the very otherness which had newly inspirited and enlivened them, and made me aware of how poor they are now to embody praise and community. This isn't the whole story, of course. The writer himself can never know the whole story; he can only see a little of what he is telling, between beginnings.

September 1980